Live Your Dream: An 8 Step Guide to Transform Your Dream to Reality

Sachin Medhi

Warning—Disclaimer

This book is designed to provide information on ways a person can achieve their dreams into physical reality by applying practical techniques in day-to-day life. It is sold with the understanding that the publisher and author are not engaged in rendering legal, accounting, or other professional services. If legal or other expert assistance is required, the services of a competent professional should be sought.

You are urged to read all the available material, learn as much as possible about converting dreams to reality and tailor the information to your individual needs.

Every effort has been made to make this book as complete and as accurate as possible. However, there may be mistakes, both typographical and in content. Therefore, this text should be used only as a general guide and not as the ultimate source for converting dreams to reality.

Furthermore, this book contains information on some practical tool and techniques one can use to convert dream into reality that is current only up to the printing date. The purpose of this book is to educate and entertain. The author shall have neither liability nor responsibility to any person or entity with respect to any loss or damage caused, or alleged to have been caused, directly or indirectly, by the information contained in this book.

If you do not wish to be bound by the above, you may return this book to the publisher for a full refund

DEDICATION

Dedicated to my loving wife Amruta and my son Kaveesh, my father Late Prabhakar Medhi, my mother Padma Medhi.

This page intentionally left blank

CONTENTS

This page intentionally left blank

ACKNOWLEDGMENTS

I thank my son Kaveesh for teaching me how to be enthusiastic, how to keep the child in me alive and how to keep asking questions till I get an answer. I thank my wife Amruta for providing me all the support while writing this book and renewing my interest in learning new things. I want to thank my father Late. Prabhakar Medhi for teaching me excellent summarizing skills and providing me the motivation to read more books. I want to thank my mother Padma Medhi for teaching me patience and importance of reading religious books for seeking answers. I also want to thank my in-laws, Gopal Sane for teaching me to focus on one thing at a time and Neelima Sane for teaching me on how to care for multiple things at same time

I offer my gratitude and prayers to Lord Ganpati for wonderful things in all aspects of my life. I also want to thank my spiritual teachers for teaching me how to connect to inner self. Special thanks to Master Zhi Gang Sha for teaching me 10 Greatest Tao Qualities of Love, Forgiveness, Compassion, Light, Humility, Harmony, Flourishing, Gratitude, Service and Enlightenment

I also want to thank readers who read this book.

Thank   You,   Thanks   You,   Thank   You!

This page intentionally left blank

0 INTRODUCTION

Do you drive a vehicle? Think of a ride/drive you went on and enjoyed a lot. You were enjoying the ride. It was nice and smooth ride with your vehicle moving at full speed. You were enjoying the fast-moving trees, the road and things on the road. It was so nice and swift feeling. Suddenly you see a roadblock. "SCREEEEEECH!" "SCREEEEEECH!" "SCREEEEEECH!" You had to brake/stop because of a roadblock? What was that feeling? Did you feel frustrated, angry, anguished?

Have you faced such roadblocks in your journey as a to Live Your Dream? Let us look at 8 steps which helped me to overcome the roadblock and Live My Dream life.

How to use this book?

Read this book once from start to finish for sake of completeness. After that assess which steps you need to work on. Maintain your own separate journal and write down your experiences. Be innovative, proactive and use your imagination as best as you can.

1 SECOND ONE: OVERVIEW AND FARMING PRINCIPLE

Okay, so today we are going to talk about seven principles or seven steps that will help you to achieve whatever is your goal or whatever is your target. Now these seven principles are nothing new. They are available all around the world. They are available in everything that you want to do. Basically, even if you want to go from point A to point B travel or if you want to cook a good meal or if you want to do something good in your job everywhere, these principles are available and you can use these to achieve your

Physical health, your spiritual mental health, your financial goals, your relationship goals, all of it. You can apply these principles universally. These are things which you can apply in every part and parcel of your life to what level of degree you need to apply that is dependent on the goal that you want to achieve. So, what are the seven principles? These seven principles is what I followed to have a great success in my life. And of course, there were failures as well. So depending on the situation, depending on the circumstances, depending on the decisions I made at that time, these principles have always helped me to achieve the goals. And whenever there were failures to achieve the goals, it was because I applied the principle wrongly or it was based on the circumstances that I was facing at that particular time. As I said, success is 99% hard work, 1% luck. So that 1% luck plays a big factor sometimes. So these principles are basically called on in simple limit terms. I have tried to put them first is the farm principle. Second is where you are currently. So the starting point then where do you want to go? So the endpoint, how are you going to go from point A to point B? So how we are going to achieve the goal, combining these all three factors together. So you cannot think of all these three things in isolation. You have to combine them all together.

Then you have to list actions,

Daily, weekly, monthly actions that are needed to achieve whatever you want to achieve. And then last point is you have to review it all together every week or based on a frequency that you want to do. So this is all about those seven principles. We'll deep dive into each of them and there's a chapter dedicated for each of these principles and how you want can achieve what you want to achieve using these principles as I call them. So let's jump into the first one. The first chapter is farm principle. So what do I mean by a farm principle? The farm principle is simple, right? Human being and human started living on earth. First. Human used to go into forest and eat whatever was there on the trees, the fruits, the vegetables that were there grown in the forest or maybe use the animals to have satisfied the needs of milk or meat or fish. So basically, it wasn't unarranged or unplanned or it was basically not very planned kind of food that human being used to eat. But when the civilization started, humans realized that if they do farming, then it is much easier to repeatedly grow whatever they want. And that is this principle all about. So basically, you take seeds,

You prepare the farm for the seeds, then you sow the seeds, you nurture them, you take care of them, water them, put plant food or fertilizers, whatever is needed to grow, and then take good care of them, give them good sun so that they can grow, take care of any pest or any insects that will harm the crop.

And at the end of the season, you take the crop and go and sell it in the market or maybe use it for your domestic needs. So that is what this farming principle is all about. You basically sow a seed and you take care of the seed, take care of the plant, and you reap the benefit. So on similar lines, whatever thoughts we are having, those are all seeds. So now these seeds, if you plant positive and good seeds, you get a positive and good crop. If you plant negative and wrong seeds, you get again, a negative or a wrong crop. So thoughts are things. So I read it somewhere, I believe it is again in seven Habits. That is one of the good books which I had read. Seven Habits of Highly Effective People by Stephen. So whatever you are sowing, that is what crop is going to come out. If you take a mango seed and then if you sow a mango seed, then there is a mango tree that is going to grow out of it, and there cannot be any apple tree going out of it. It's as simple as that. So even if you offer the plant, same food, same water, the d n of the plant or the basic genetics of the plant always decides what kind of crop is going to grow out of it. So in similar lines, if your initial thought idea or your initial goal is very clear and

You exactly know what you want then and because much easier to get the crop out of it. Because if the seed is

Of a positive nature of a clear nature, then you get a good plant out of it, and then you take care of it. You nurture the seed and you nurture the thought, and you grow it into an idea, grow it into a complete process. You implement the process and then you reap a good benefit out of it. So that is the whole idea behind the farming principle. And again, as in case of a farm, you have to take care of it day in, day out, every hour of the day. You have to take care of it, you have to protect it, you have to nurture it, you have to water it, you have to give it food, fertilizers, whatever you want to call it. You have to make sure it gets enough sun, there is nourishment. And then once the plant is ready, you take the benefit or you

Reap the crop, right? You cannot leave the crop as it is when the plant is ready to give its fruits. You go and use the fruits or whatever the crop you have on time, because if you keep it as it is, then it'll be wasted. Fruits won't stay fresh forever. So you have to also rip the benefits from the crop on time. So that is very important as well. Sometimes we forget to rip the benefits, we take the complete care to grow the crop, but then at the end of the day, we don't take the benefits out of it. So this is the farming principle in a nutshell. We'll deep dive into each of it, each of the steps that are needed for farming principle, and then

See what is needed to grow your goal into a big crop. We'll think on those lines as well. Another reason why I like the farming principle is once you have the farm, once you have it all ready, you can take multiple crops on it. So once the platform is ready, once you have everything ready, what you need to do is you just need to change the thoughts that you're going to plant in the farm. So basically, I call it as the farm of the business or farm of the life. And then you plot different, you sow different seeds, different thought, different ideas, and then take the benefit out of each every time. But the process to nurture the farm or to grow the crop that remains the same. There are two aspects to it. So basically, you have a different seed with the, that will cue you a different crop or a different thought that will give you a different idea or a different process. But what you need to understand is the process to grow the crop from the thought or from grow a business, from an idea, or to grow a dream into reality. The process remains the same. So that is very important for you to understand. But once that is very clear, what you can do is you can use the same process repeatedly and achieve your goals, achieve your dreams.

2 SECOND STEP: FARMING PRINCIPLE IN DETAIL

This is a story about farming principle. I was about eight or ten years old, and my father brought me some seeds from the market. He wanted to plant some seeds in our house. We had a small garden in our balcony. We used to stay on the first floor at that time. There was a small garden which he had prepared. And at that time, he was sowing the seeds and I, of course, I was very enthusiastic about what he's doing. Therefore, I go over there and I ask him, "Father, what are you doing?" He tells me that "Son, I'm planting a seed, and after two or three months, the seed will grow into a plant and it'll give beautiful flowers. There will be flowers which will grow on the tree, on the plant, and you can then use these flowers either to offer them to God or for the decorations in the house. That's why I'm planting the seeds."

I was very enthusiastic about it because I had seen plants and trees around me. But when he was planting the tree, I mean the plant, I was very enthusiastic about it because I wanted to see how the seed grew into a plant and what all things were needed to do it. I asked him, "Father, how do you plant the seed and what all things are needed to take care of it, to grow it into a plant?" Then my father

tells me- "Basically what you need is, of course, you need a plant and you need a plant in your mind." So, what plant you want to grow. He told me that it was a flowering plant,

yellow coloured, I don't remember the name of the plant exactly, it was long time back. So, he tells me that this is a flowering plant and it has yellow-coloured flowers. And I sow some seeds and they were brown colour seeds.

And I'm seeing at the seeds and I'm thinking, okay, so this particular seed is off yellow colour. So how does the plant know that it'll have yellow colour seeds? That was a very question for a very young mind. I was not aware of the D N A and the genetics at that time. I studied about them later in my life, during my high school. I was thinking, how will the plant know that the flower colour has to be yellow? Or what shape should be the flower, or how many petals would be there in the flower?

I ask all these questions to my father, and he told me that the seed is kind of a data bank. So, the seed has all the information that is needed for the plant to grow, and it also has the sufficient nutrition that is needed for the initial sprout to grow out of the seed once you have to offer water. And then there is sunlight, and then there is soil. Thus, these three things will help the plan to grow: the sunlight, the soil, and the water. And then a small sprout will come out of the seed, we will take care of it, and then it'll grow into a plant.

I was very enthusiastic about it, as I said earlier, and I wanted to see that whole plant grow in front of my eyes.

My father dug a small hole in the soil and then planted the seeds over there and of course, nourished it with water. Therefore, poured some water over the soil, made it wet and kept it wet. Every day, every morning, once I used to wake up, I used to go out and see whether there is a sprout has grown to the seed, because this was the first seed which I had seen being planted. After three or four days, there was a small green coloured sprout, which came out of the seed, and I was very happy about it. I went to my father and said, "Father, Father, the seed has grown into a small sprout, and can you please come and look? He was very supporting of me. He went along with me, though it was a small thing.

He went along with me and just saw that sprout because he knew that though it was a small thing in day-to-day life, it was a very big thing for me. He went along with me and we saw that sprout over there. And then once the sprout came out, I knew that the seed will grow into a plant because the initial step has already been taken by the plant to convert it into a sprout, for it was just a seed. If you kept it in a paper bag or in a drawer or somewhere where it is not in soil, it is just a seed. But once you take the seed and put it in soil, put that pot in sunlight and pour some water over it, a sprout has to come out of the seed. That is the whole process.

I was very much overwhelmed to see the process because that is how nature grows. You take a seed, you give it the proper conditions, and then there will be a plant that will grow out of the seed. That is very the natural process, and that is how nature grows. Therefore, on the similar lines, I was thinking that is also true with the thought, right? You take a thought, you give it proper nourishment, you give it proper conditions, you apply the proper principles, water it, nurture it, give it the sunlight it needs. And then that thought will grow into an idea. It'll grow into maybe a business, it might go into a personal victory, it might go into a challenge that you want to overcome, and you take the steps one step at a time and it'll grow into a plant. All the organizations, all the big companies, all the things that you see in this world, which are created by human being, all have started from a small idea, maybe the wheel of the car or
may be a big rocket.

Everything started with a small idea. There were proper conditions applied to it, proper nourishment, proper watering, proper sunlight. And that idea has grown into a big tree over the period of time.

And with many big trees, it can grow into forest. So that's the natural principle I was talking about, the farming principle. You take one plant, you take one seed at a time, grow it into a plant, add multiple seeds. Once you grow them into a plant, it can turn into trees and it can turn into a forest.

Coming back to my first seed sprouting experience, right after one week or so, there was first leaf that came out. And then in 15 days' time, there were multiple leaves on that plant, and I used to take care of it. I used to water it. I asked my father that, how much water should I put because I don't want to drown it into water. So he gave me a small bowl with some markings, and I used to pour that much water. And when this plant started growing, we increased the water by that much amount, whatever was extra needed, because once the thing starts growing, you need to give extra nourishment.

You cannot have, the initial nourishment has to increase, right? And then after three months or so, the plant really grew into a big that will multiple branches out of it. And then I saw nice big flowers on it one day. And there was, of course, there were buds first. And then on third or fourth day, the buds grew into flowers, and those were nice
yellow flowers, which we offer to our God. Those flowers were very beautiful, very nice fragrance. And my father told me, see if you take care of things and if you take care of them consistently over a period of time and give them proper nourishment, seeds, can grow into a plant, plant can grow into a tree, and they can give you valuable fruits, valuable flowers; and the fragrance of the flowers, the taste of the fruit will be sweet.
That will be your end goal to nurture a seed, turn it into a plant or a tree, and it'll give you fruits and flowers. That's the nature's way to grow. This is the farming principle.

And once you know the farming principle, you know that if you have an idea, you have a proper idea in your mind, you grow that proper idea, nourish it properly, and it can grow into a plant, a tree, into a multiple such trees, you can make a forest out of it.

What happened after two and a half months when this plant was flowering, I saw some weeds that had grown out over there near the plant. I asked my father that, how

come these weeds came out way? We did not plant any
seeds or any weeds over there.

Then my father told the weeds were there in the soil,
which we were using because we were nurturing the plant.
The weeds also need same kind of nourishment and the
weeds grow.

I asked my father that, what is the best way to get rid of
the weeds? He told me that first you make sure that there
are no seeds of weeds or if the weeds grow, you have to
pluck them out when they are very small, when they're
very
tiny, because the bigger they grow, the difficult it becomes
to up root them, to remove them. And then they will take
the nourishment from the flowering plant. And the
flowering plant may dry out and you may not get the
flowers at all.

Therefore, the farming principle is applicable for
good thoughts as well as bad thoughts or good seeds, as
well
as bad seeds.

Unless and until you stop negative thoughts,
negative seeds, bad seeds out of your own garden, you may
get weeds in the garden. The best way to do it is have
proper thoughts, positive thoughts, positive seeds, positive
emotions, and give them proper nourishment to grow
them into flowering plants.

Plants, which will give you beautiful flowers, which will
give you sweet fruits. Otherwise, weeds will always grow.

Weeds will take over your garden, and if weeds come
in, they come in bundle, they come in mass, and once they
grow, it is very difficult to uproot them because they turn
into strong trees as well.

So, whenever you are having any thoughts, just make
sure that you are having all the positive thoughts and there
is nothing negative that you are nurturing, that you are
growing in your mind. Because your mind is the farm.
Thoughts are the seeds and your daily habits or the daily

actions that you take on these thoughts are nothing but the sunlight, the water, and the soil or the nourishment that is needed for the thought to grow.

Therefore, whenever you are having bad thoughts, take some time off or maybe five, ten minutes and just ease down. Just understand that those thoughts needs to be cleaned over there. It's done and there itself.

So how do you do it? You can either use your past good memories to overcome the negative thoughts, or you can read some good books or you can do meditation.

There are hundreds of ways to do it. You have to figure out your own way. But whenever you're having wrong thoughts, you have to tell your mind to stop, and you have to go again into the good thoughts' territory, as I call it. Because once you have good thoughts, you get good seeds, and then you get good plants and you get a good tree, you get a good forest out of your garden will be absolutely flourishing with good things in your life.

This is the farming principle. Farming principle is not only applicable on earth, it is also applicable in your mind, and your mind is unlimited. It has unlimited potential.

If you put your mind to good thoughts, to good seeds, you will definitely grow good plants, good trees out of it.

This is very important and this is where the difference between leadership and management comes.

Management is all about growing plants or trees from the seeds. While leadership is all about choosing the right seeds, so choose right seeds and you'll have good yield or good crop out of it. This is the farming principle, which I was wanted to tell you about and apply this in your life and on daily basis, and it'll help you.

Outline of the Chapter
- **Farming Principle Story – Key Take Aways**

- Introduction to the story of planting seeds
- The process of planting and nurturing the seed
- Comparing the growth of a seed to the growth of an idea or thought
- The importance of proper nourishment and conditions for growth
- The concept of weeds and the need to remove negative thoughts
- Applying the farming principle to the mind and personal growth
- Techniques for overcoming negative thoughts
- The difference between leadership and management in relation to the farming principle

Actions from the Chapter

1. Nurture positive thoughts and avoid negative thoughts.
2. Take time to clean and clear negative thoughts from your mind.
3. Use past good memories or engage in activities like reading or meditation to overcome negative thoughts.
4. Choose the right seeds (positive thoughts) to plant in your mind.
5. Stop negative thoughts and redirect your mind towards positive thoughts.
6. Apply the farming principle to your thoughts by providing them with proper nourishment, such as

good habits and actions.

7. Understand that ideas and thoughts, like seeds, have the potential to grow into something bigger with the right conditions and nourishment.

8. Take care of your thoughts consistently over time to see them grow into ideas, projects, or personal victories.

9. Be aware of and remove any negative thoughts or "weeds" that may hinder the growth of positive thoughts.

10. Remember that the farming principle applies to both positive and negative thoughts, so it is important to actively cultivate positive thoughts and remove negative ones.

Activities That Can Help You

Some suggested activities to implement the action points provided in the context could include:

1. **Practicing positive thinking:** Take 5-10 minutes each day to consciously focus on positive thoughts and let go of negative thoughts. This can be done through meditation, reading uplifting books, or reflecting on past good memories.

2. **Nurturing good thoughts**: Treat your mind like a garden and consciously choose to nurture positive thoughts. This can be done by surrounding yourself with positive influences, engaging in activities that bring you joy, and practicing gratitude.

3. **Identifying and removing negative thoughts:** When negative thoughts arise, acknowledge them and consciously redirect your focus to positive

thoughts. Use techniques like visualization, affirmations, or journaling to help shift your mindset.

4. **Applying the farming principle:** Apply the concept of the farming principle to your goals and ideas. Take one idea at a time, nourish it with proper conditions (research, planning, action), and watch it grow into a tangible outcome. Consistency and patience are key.

5. **Consistently nurturing and nourishing ideas:** Just like plants need consistent care and nourishment to grow, consistently invest time and effort into your ideas. This can involve setting goals, creating action plans, seeking feedback, and adapting as needed.

6. **Recognizing and removing "weeds":** Be aware of negative influences or thoughts that can hinder your progress. Actively identify and remove these "weeds" from your mind and environment. This may involve distancing yourself from negative people, limiting exposure to negative media, or practicing self-reflection to address limiting beliefs.

7. **Increasing nourishment for growth:** As your ideas or projects start to grow, increase your efforts and resources to support their development. This can include seeking additional knowledge or skills, investing more time and energy, or seeking support from mentors or experts.

Remember, these are just suggestions, and it's important to find what works best for you.

Experiment with different activities and techniques to find the ones that resonate with you and support your personal growth and development.

Examples of Massive Actions That You Can Take

1. **Practice positive thinking**: Take 5-10 minutes each day to reflect on positive memories or experiences. Write them down in a gratitude journal or share them with a friend or family member.

2. **Read uplifting books:** Set aside time each day to read books that inspire and motivate you. Choose books that align with your interests and goals, whether it's self-help, personal development, or biographies of successful individuals.

3. **Meditation:** Incorporate meditation into your daily routine. Find a quiet and comfortable space, close your eyes, and focus on your breath. Allow any negative thoughts to pass by without judgment and bring your attention back to the present moment.

4. **Stop negative thoughts:** When you catch yourself having negative thoughts, consciously interrupt them and replace them with positive affirmations or thoughts. Remind yourself of your strengths, accomplishments, and the things you are grateful for.

5. **Choose the right seeds:** Reflect on your goals and aspirations. Identify the thoughts and beliefs that align with those goals and consciously choose

to nurture and cultivate those positive thoughts.

6.   **Take small steps:** Break down your goals into smaller, manageable tasks. Take one step at a time and celebrate each small achievement along the way. This will help you stay motivated and build momentum towards your larger goals.

7.   **Weed out negative influences:** Identify any negative influences or toxic relationships in your life. Take steps to distance yourself from these influences and surround yourself with positive and supportive people who uplift and inspire you.

Remember, these are just examples, and it's important to find activities that resonate with you personally. Experiment with different practices and find what works best for you in cultivating positive thoughts and actions

3 THIRD STEP: WHERE YOU ARE?

This is the story about where you are. The current situation that you are in or the current lifestyle that you have or the current problems that we are facing. This is story about that. I'll share with you one incident in my life. I believe it was when I started working in my career and I met one of my colleagues who was there in the industry. He was working in IT industry for a very long time. He took me to a coffee, just a casual talk, and we were just discussing some things, some problem related to our work, how to solve one of the problems related to computers, because I work in IT field. We were discussing that and then the discussion suddenly went into understanding each other. And then he told me, look, Sachin, I will tell you one of the greatest things that I learned, and he shared this very nice thing with me. He told me that to become a millionaire, you need $1 million or whatever, 1 million pounds in your bank account, right? A person who is a millionaire, of course has to have the million dollars or million pounds or whatever the currency in the bank account. It could be either in liquid form or you could have a house or you could have an office. Basically, either to have $1 million or pounds in liquid or to have them as an investment, you need to have that amount. You need to earn that amount. He was saying there are at least 10 different ways of making a million dollars, but these 10 different ways will remain the same across all the businesses. I was wondering how is that possible? I asked him: Hey, can you tell me how it is possible that there are 10 different ways, but these ways remain common across all the businesses. Even if I'm working in an insurance company, I'm working in it, I'm working as a sportsman. Whatever the way or whatever, the earning way I have these methods remain the same. I did not understand that part. He told me one very simple thing. He told me to earn a million dollars or pounds, you need to sell a product, which is of $1 million or pounds. I said, yeah, that is very true. Then he said that there are multiple ways of selling this product. You either take one product where the value of the product is a million dollars and then you sell it to one person. That is one way. Second is you create 10 different products each bringing you a revenue of a hundred thousand, and then you add it, and then those 10 products into a hundred thousand each become a million. Similarly, if you have a $10,000 product, then you have to sell it a hundred times. So, so far, so good. Basically, what he was trying to tell me is you have a product which is a good product, which is a quality product, which really solves a problem, and then you have to sell it that many number of times with whatever is the unit cost that you have, and that's the only way to earn a million dollars. I was really amazed at it because if you are a product owner or if you sell products, and if you are a product owner or if you have a service, if you sell services or consultancy, then you have to do it.

You have to use the same formula again and again. Basically, you have to have a product and you have to sell it that many number of times too, to make a million dollars. This is what really triggered one thought in me that where I am currently, because this was completely different perspective of life, this was not taught to me in my school even that did not teach me this in college. So this person who has got good experience of life, he gives me this simple trick, a simple breakdown, a simple mathematics of $1 million, which was never told to me, means everyone used. It's a simple sum, right? Actually a hundred multiplied by a hundred is 10,000 and 10,000 multiplied by a hundred is a million. It is a simple sum.

I had done this mathematics in my class, in my college,
but I never thought it in this way that if I have a sales
product, if I sell a product of that much value, that
many number of times, then I can earn big amount of
money.

That was the general idea. The current knowledge I
have or the current skills I have or the current
learnings I have, the current mindset I have is the
reason why I am where I am currently. My current
position, my current situation in my life, the current
problems which I have in my life are all because of
whatever I have learned, whatever skills I have earned
and whatever knowledge I have applied to a situation
till my current time. And if that is very good, then I
will be in a better position. But of course, as I said,
this is farming principle as I keep on saying that. I
need to grow the tree or the plant needs to grow. If I
don't grow, then I will dry out. If I want to now go
ahead in my life, I need to have a new learning, have a
new skill, apply that knowledge skill, take the massive
action that is needed to break out of my current
comfort zone and then go to a newer way of living or
newer way of working, basically it is a really simple
thing.

That story told me or that conversation with that
colleague told me that whatever you are currently
doing that directly impacts the life that you're going to
live after next one year, two years, three years, five
years. So whatever time I'm spending currently on day-
to-day basis, on hourly basis, on every minute that I'm
spending today, how I spend it decides what life I live
in, my future, in my near future. The current or the
present tense decides the future tense. And why I am
having this current position is because of my past
tense or whatever I have learned in past, whatever
knowledge I have, whatever mindset I have, whatever
skills I have, it is because of those or whatever habits I

have because of those. If I want to go to a newer level, then I need to break old habits which are not giving me anything and develop new habits.

You have to understand it in that way. Whatever my daily, weekly, monthly task I do, whatever my daily, weekly, monthly habits I have, whatever the daily, weekly, monthly thinking I have, that is the reason I am there in my current situation. And if I'm going to change it, if I'm going to start applying the growth principles of nature, then I will definitely change my situation. That is what this story is all about. Why we are in current situation, there are three reasons for it. Whatever things we have learned so far, whatever skills or knowledge we have and whatever mindset we have, if you try changing these three basic things, then all others doors will automatically open for you the newer doors, and you will go in a new dimension in your life, a new phase in your life, so you will see changes happening in your life. The amount of change you do in your daily, weekly, monthly activities will directly tell the amount of changes, transformations, or the new way of life that you're going to live that is going to come in future.

That is all the story is all about. I am really thankful to that colleague for opening my eyes and telling me this breakup of how to earn a million dollars or a million pounds and how to think about it. One of the very important things she taught me was you have to sell yourself your skills, your products, your services, whatever things you're going to offer that you have to sell. Unless and until you sell it, no one is going to know about it and no one is going to buy it unless and until anyone is going to buy it. No one is going to pay you. There's a very simple math and a very simple logic, and if you apply that in your life, it really helps. And this is not only true for earning money, this is also true for earning anything. If you want to have a good health or good relationships, you have to spend time.

You have to understand for health why you are at current position. It might not be all under your control because you might have some things which are out of your control, but instead of blaming yourself or others for what you have, if you objectively think about it and try to see how you can become better in the current situation, how you can face it, then it'll be much easier. And in terms of relationships, as I said earlier, I read this line somewhere, slow is fast and fast is slow. I believe it is in Stephen Co seven Habits of Highly Effective People. In relationships, you have to put it in that way. You have to understand it from other person's perspective. So first, seek to understand, then be understood. Again, this is from Stephen Covey, The Seven Habits of Highly Effective People or one of the things which I learned over there, that to understand other person's perspective and then you have to explain your perspective and that will help you improve the relationship.

This learning, which I had from the colleague is applicable in all walks of life or all aspects of life. How much is dependent on how we apply the principle, how we apply the learnings for that particular situation. It's directly dependent on that. And if you apply it correctly, chances are bright or the situation will change, the chances are very bright on applying the learnings as you know them. That is all about the story and just be aware of where you are. It is called as situational report., I believe, in situational report. My current situational report. is as What is my current situational report? that will tell you why it is my current situational report. It's a snapshot of the life on all the dimensions that you think finances, relationships, and your health. You can break all the other goals into these three major categories and then see where you are.

You can rate yourself and just keep that rating to you. For example, health-wise, maybe exercising. I am at one. On the scale of one to 10, because I don't do any exercise at all, I might be on the scale of eight out of 10 because I have got good savings to take care of my life. And in terms of relationship, each relationship, you can again rate it based on your perspective. Maybe I am good with one relationship, maybe I am eight out of 10, but for some other relationship I might be two out of 10. Depending on that, you can prepare a score card for yourself. Because if you have numbers then the numbers talk louder and the numbers will tell you where you are. But again, very important thing, numbers are not reflection of you. It is just one way to measure it. It is not a reflection of you. You can always change as a person. So don't be too much bound by it. It is just a measuring parameter to know because if you measure, then it becomes easier for you to change the situation and don't go by the numbers too much, just make sure that you know where you are. That awareness is there. Then that is half the battle won already. This is all about where I am currently.

Key Take Aways from the Chapter

1. To become a millionaire, you need to sell a product or service worth a million dollars or pounds.

2. There are multiple ways to sell a million-dollar product, such as selling one product to one person or selling multiple products at a lower price.

3. Your current situation is a result of your past learnings, skills, mindset, and habits.

4. To change your current situation, you need to break

old habits and develop new ones.

5. The amount of change you make in your daily, weekly, and monthly activities will determine the changes and transformations you experience in the future.

6. Selling yourself, your skills, products, or services is crucial for success in any area of life.

7. Understanding and seeking to understand others' perspectives is important for building and improving relationships.

8. It's important to be aware of your current situation in all aspects of life, such as finances, relationships, and health.

9. Rating yourself on different aspects of life can help you identify areas for improvement.

10. Numbers are just a measuring parameter and not a reflection of your worth as a person.

Actions you can implement

1. **Evaluate your current situation:** Take some time to reflect on your current habits, skills, knowledge, and mindset. Assess where you are in terms of your finances, relationships, and health. This self-awareness will help you understand why you are in your current situation.

2. **Identify areas for improvement:** Once you have evaluated your current situation, identify areas where you can make changes and improvements. This could involve acquiring new skills, gaining more knowledge, or changing your mindset.

3. **Set goals:** Determine what you want to achieve in the future. Set specific, measurable, achievable, relevant, and time-bound goals in areas such as finances,

relationships, and health. This will give you a clear direction to work towards.

4. **Take action:** Start implementing the necessary changes and taking steps towards your goals. This could involve learning new skills, seeking personal development opportunities, building better relationships, or adopting healthier habits.

5. **Monitor your progress**: Regularly assess your progress towards your goals. Keep track of your actions and measure your success. Adjust your approach if needed and stay committed to your growth and improvement.

Activities That Can Help You

Some activities that can help you make changes and improvements in your life include:

1. **Setting goals:** Clearly define what you want to achieve and create a plan to work towards those goals.

2. **Self-reflection:** Take time to reflect on your current situation, identify areas for improvement, and understand your strengths and weaknesses.

3. **Learning and acquiring new skills:** Continuously seek knowledge and develop new skills that are relevant to your goals and interests.

4. **Taking action:** Implement the knowledge and skills you have acquired by taking consistent and purposeful action towards your goals.

5. **Building positive habits:** Identify habits that

support your goals and work on incorporating them into your daily routine.

6. Seeking feedback: Be open to receiving feedback from others and use it as an opportunity for growth and improvement.

7. **Surrounding yourself with positive influences:** Surround yourself with people who inspire and motivate you to become the best version of yourself.

8. **Practicing self-care:** Take care of your physical, mental, and emotional well-being by engaging in activities that promote relaxation, stress reduction, and overall health.

9. **Embracing challenges and setbacks:** View challenges and setbacks as opportunities for growth and learning rather than obstacles.

10. **Celebrating achievements:** Acknowledge and celebrate your progress and achievements along the way to stay motivated and inspired.

How internet has changed the world?

The concept of creating and selling products applies to the internet in a similar way as it does in traditional business. The internet provides a platform for individuals and businesses to reach a wider audience and sell their products or services online. This can be done through e-commerce websites, online marketplaces, social media platforms, or even through digital downloads.

Creating and selling products on the internet requires identifying a target market, developing a product that meets their needs or solves a problem, and then marketing and promoting the product to reach potential customers. The internet offers various tools and strategies for marketing and selling products, such as search engine optimization (SEO), social media advertising, email marketing, and content marketing.

Additionally, the internet allows for the creation and sale of digital products, such as e-books, online courses, software, and digital artwork. These products can be easily distributed and accessed by customers worldwide, providing opportunities for scalability and global reach.

Overall, the internet provides a vast marketplace for individuals and businesses to create and sell products, reaching a larger audience and potentially generating significant   revenue.

4 FOURTH STEP: WHERE YOU WANT TO BE?

Okay, so where you want to be, this is a story about where you want to be. And I was in the ninth grade in my school when this story occurred in my life, when this story happened in my life. So what happened is I was in the ninth grade, I believe it was somewhere a month of our annual celebrations in the school. And a lot of annual activities happened over the course of the celebration. So there was a sports day, then there was annual cultural events where students used to participate in dramas and singing or the stage, and then there was a fun fare. And at the end there was also prize distribution. Now, this prize distribution was not only for the events in the sports day or the cultural event, but also in the academics. So whoever was doing good in academics, they were awarded like the first prize for the highest mask score in a subject or best students award, or person who has stood with the first rank in the school, second rank in the school, or the third rank.

So basically, toppers used to get all the academic

awards topper in the sports, used to get all the sports
awards, and of course the cultural event operas, drama and
singing competition winners used to get prizes from that
particular category. So I'm sitting in this nine standard
ninth grade annual prize distribution, and I have around
40, 45 students studying with me in my class. So, they were
calling out names. My teachers were calling out the names
for the prizes, and it was based on grade. So first to get the
fifth grade, sixth grade, seventh grade, so eighth grade,
ninth grade. And then when the ninth-grade name came,
my friend got a prize for scoring best marks in
mathematics. Another friend got a prize to score best
marks in languages like English, Marathi, Hindi. Some of
my other friends got good awards because they stood first
in running race or in cricket. They were best in scoring
runs or some of them were best in other sports like
basketball. And some of my friends got good awards
because of their singing talent or because of their dancing
talent. And after the event ended, I did not get any awards.
I was

Not any awards at that time. So, one of my senior
friends from 10th grade, he came to me and he said,
Sachin, how come you are not having any awards? I said,
maybe I was not good enough. So, I did not get any
awards in any of the categories. So, then this friend tells
me, ah, don't worry. It's okay to not get any awards. What
you can do is you can try it next time. 10th. 10th is the last
grade. So in my schooling, we call the 10th grade or the
10th year class was the final class of the school. And there
is a big exam which is conducted at the state level, and that
is the last year of the school. So, after that, you of course
go to the junior college. So, you go to your 11 standard
and your 12 standard, as we call it back in my country.

So, this friend tells me that, don't worry, you can always
stress there is always a next year. So don't be too much,
don't feel too bad about it. So I came home and thinking,
right, don't feel bad about it is fine, but at least I have my

emotions. How can I not feel bad about it? Because I did not win a single award or single prize during that year, and I had taken efforts, but I did not win. So, then I was thinking why I did not win that year, and I was sleepless that night. So I was thinking about it for the whole night, why I was not getting any awards because I had tried things. I had because I was good at academics. I was not so very good at sports, but I gave it a try. And for cultural events also, I had participated in multiple events during that ninth grade, but then it suddenly clicked me, yes, you have done good things, but they were not the excellent things.

They were not the best things. And if they were not the best things, you may not have got the award that year or you may not get a prize. So, then I think about this, right? If I am outstanding in my own sense, then we'll make a difference. Because done is better than perfect is always true. Done is better than perfect is always true. But sometimes you have to also go to the level where you achieve something. You have fulfilled something. So, I was thinking that what all things I want to achieve and then it suddenly clicked me. When I started my previous years grade school, I was not having the goal. I did not think that what I should be achieving at the end of the year and this lack of clarity is what had costed me that day because I was not sure where I should excel or what I should have that caused the whole problem because I was not knowing where I want to be.

The end goal was not very clear. I knew that I had to excel, I need that. I had to perform good at various academic subjects, at various cultural activities, but I was not definite that out of these subjects, these are the subjects or these are the academic areas where I have to be the best or these are the cultural activities or sports activities where I have to be the best. That clarity was not there. And because that clarity was not there, because that end goal was not there, I did not win any prizes that night and I had a sleepless night. So then what I did is I decided that next year I figured out based on my scoring that which are my best subjects. So of course, I always used to love mathematics and science in the school. I was also very good at languages, but mathematic science, history, geography, where my strength areas, those were my very strong areas and languages were bit on a back burner.

So, I decided that at least these three areas, I will excel next year and I will give my best next year. I did not compare myself with my friends, I compared myself with me. This is very important. You compare yourself with you. You don't compare yourself with the world, otherwise you will never excel because world, there will be always people in the world who are far ahead of you, who are far behind you. So if you do that comparison, you are never going to get a proper measurement. To get a proper measurement, you need a benchmark and the benchmark has to be you. So what was your previous performance and what is your next performance? If you do those two comparisons, that is the best measurement that you can get and that's the most correct measurement that you can get. So I decided that in my ninth grade, in these three subjects, these four subjects, history, geography, science and mathematics, this is what I have scored and I should at

Least score this much in my next grade. And then I started preparing accordingly. And for cultural and sport activities, I decided that I will try to excel into the running race because I was good at running. And then I will also try to excel into drama because I was also good at performing drama at that time. So these two areas I will focus on, but the main focus was academic. Because I was very academic, I used to love studying all the subjects. So that was the primary area. So then my primary goal was to excel in these four subjects, history, geography, mathematics, science. The secondary goal was to excel into the drama. And the additional goal or the good thing to achieve was to excel in running as well. So I started working on it and I started putting out my daily activities to make sure that my daily activities are aligned to my goals.

And during my last year, the 10th grade, I started very hard. I used to wake up early in the morning. I used to study. I used to go to classes, take the proper coaching needed in these subjects, then accordingly take care of working throughout the day or the subjects in the evening. I used to also focus on my running and as well as on my drama things, I used to act in front of mirror. So, what happened is after one year when the award ceremony came or the prize distribution evening came, I was getting called for each and every prize. So, I excelled. I was best in mathematics, I was best in science, I was best in history, geography, and I was the topper in two of them. And I was the second person in mathematics. So, I excelled. I was in top three in all these three areas.

Of course, the running race I lost. And in the drama we did, I believe it was some small play from movie. It's a very famous movie in my country. So I played a small role in that. But of course I did not win anything in the sports and the drama part of it, but at least I got good number of prizes in my academics. And that night when I slept, I was feeling very peaceful because I had gone through the pain one year back where I did not have any prizes or any awards. And come this one year, I decided what I wanted exactly. I had the clarity, I took the steps to achieve the goals I did achieve the goals, and all these awards were there with me during that night. So I had a very nice peaceful sleep. And the sports thing, which I did not win any prizes, has helped me a lot because it taught me to do exercises during my life.

And then the drama thing really helped me to put forward my thoughts, what I think I can clearly express that. So those things helped me in a way in long run in my career. So basically, they rewarded me in a different manner. So once you start preparing the goal with the clarity, if you have enough clarity on your goals and then you take the daily steps that you need to take for the goals, you will achieve your goals. Whatever your goals are, the realistic goals that you have, that they will definitely achieve and there is no stopping to it. So that was the lesson, which I learned from the story, to have clarity in what you want at the end of the goal that you are planning, what's the goal and where you want to be. If you start using your imagination, then it'll help.

Key Takeaways:

- The speaker shares a personal story about not receiving any awards during a school prize distribution event.
- The lack of clarity and specific goals contributed to not winning any prizes.
- The speaker emphasizes the importance of setting clear goals and comparing oneself to their own previous performance rather than others.
- By setting clear goals and aligning daily activities with those goals, the speaker was able to excel academically and receive multiple awards the following year.
- The speaker also highlights the value of the lessons learned from participating in sports and drama, which had long-term benefits in their career.
- The key lesson learned is to have clarity in goals and take daily steps towards achieving them.

Actions You can Implement

To have clarity in goals and take daily steps towards achieving them, the following actions can be taken:

1. **Reflect on your strengths and interests**: Identify your strengths and interests to determine what goals align with them. This will help you focus on areas where you have the potential to excel.

2. **Set specific and realistic goals:** Clearly define what you want to achieve and make sure your goals are attainable within a given timeframe. Break them down into smaller, actionable steps.

3. **Prioritize your goals:** Determine which goals are most important to you and prioritize them accordingly. This will help you allocate your time and resources effectively.

4. **Create a plan:** Develop a detailed plan outlining the steps you need to take to achieve your goals. This plan should include specific actions, deadlines, and milestones to track your progress.

5. **Take consistent action:** Commit to taking daily steps towards your goals. Consistency is key in making progress and achieving success. Stay focused and motivated, even when faced with challenges or setbacks.

6. **Monitor and evaluate your progress:** Regularly assess your progress and make adjustments to your plan if necessary. This will help you stay on track and ensure that your actions are aligned with your goals.

7. **Seek support and guidance:** Surround yourself with

supportive individuals who can provide guidance and encouragement. Consider seeking mentorship or joining groups related to your goals for additional support and accountability.

Remember, clarity in goals and consistent action are essential for achieving success. Stay committed, adapt as needed, and celebrate your achievements along the way.

Activities that can help you

1. Self-reflection: Take the time to reflect on your strengths, interests, and passions. Identify what you truly want to achieve and what areas you want to excel in.

2. Goal setting: Set clear and specific goals for yourself. Determine what you want to achieve in different areas of your life, such as academics, sports, or personal development.

3. Prioritization: Prioritize your goals based on their importance and relevance to you. Focus on the goals that align with your strengths and interests.

4. Planning: Create a plan of action to achieve your goals. Break them down into smaller, manageable steps that you can take on a daily basis.

5. Time management: Manage your time effectively by allocating specific time slots for working towards your goals. Create a schedule or use a planner to stay organized and ensure you are dedicating enough time to each goal.

6. Continuous learning: Continuously seek knowledge and improve your skills in the areas related to your goals. Take courses, read books, or seek mentorship to enhance your understanding and abilities.

7. Visualization: Use visualization techniques to imagine yourself achieving your goals. Visualize the steps you need to take and the outcomes you desire, which can help motivate and guide you towards success.

8. Self-assessment: Regularly assess your progress towards your goals. Reflect on your achievements, areas of improvement, and adjust your approach if necessary.

9. Accountability: Find someone who can hold you accountable for your actions and progress. Share your goals with them and regularly update them on your progress. This can provide motivation and support.

10. Adaptability: Be open to adapting your goals and plans as needed. Life circumstances may change, and it's important to be flexible and adjust your approach accordingly.

It's important to note that these activities are based on the context provided and may vary depending on individual preferences and circumstances.

Chapter   conclusions while relating to Business

The story about setting goals and achieving success in the tenth grade can relate to business success in several ways.

Firstly, it emphasizes the importance of having clarity in your goals. Just like the speaker in the story realized that lack of clarity in their academic goals resulted in not winning any prizes, in business, having a clear vision and specific goals is crucial for success. It helps you focus your efforts and make strategic decisions that align with your objectives.

Secondly, the story highlights the significance of self-improvement and continuous learning. The speaker in the story identified their strengths and weaknesses and focused on excelling in their strong areas while also working on improving in other areas. Similarly, in business, identifying your strengths and weaknesses, and continuously developing your skills and knowledge can help you excel in your chosen field and stay competitive.

Additionally, the story emphasizes the importance of taking daily steps towards your goals. The speaker in the story mentioned how they woke up early, studied, attended classes, and practiced their talents regularly. In business, consistent effort, discipline, and perseverance are essential for achieving success. It's about taking small, actionable steps every day that contribute to your long-term goals.

Lastly, the story highlights the importance of self-comparison rather than comparing oneself to others. The speaker in the story focused on comparing their current performance with their previous performance, which provided a benchmark for improvement. In business, it's crucial to focus on your own progress and growth rather than getting caught up in comparing yourself to others. This mindset allows you to stay motivated and focused on your own journey towards success.

Overall, the story about setting goals and achieving

success in the tenth grade can serve as a reminder that clarity, self-improvement, consistent effort, and self-comparison are key elements in achieving success, both in academics and in business.

5 FIFTH STEP: HOW YOU WILL GO THERE?

Okay, so this is the story about how you will go there. So now you identified where you are, you also know where you want to go. So, you identified your source, your destination. So, you identified what is your point A and what is your point B. Now you need to identify how you are going to go from point A to point B. So, one of the easiest ways to do it is basically start breaking it down. So, if you have a very big tree, then you can climb the tree by climbing one branch and then you can reach at the top. Or even better example is if you want to basically take care of your entire house, you start with one room at a time, clear that room, then you move to the next room and you do it enough number of times you will have cleared your house or cleaned your house.

So basically, what I'm explaining over here is it's a process where you'll have to break down the problem and break it into doable steps or doable task, and then you have to do each task and then move to the next task. It could be either sequential, it could be a radio, or you can also use something no known as a sprint approach. So in sprint approach, you can do things on a four to six week basis. So INS sequential is, of course you do step one, step two, step three, all in sequences. You identify a cycle to do things like for example, if you want to do some exercises, then you identify the cycle, you identify the strength exercises, the cardiovascular exercises, and then the stretching exercises. And then you figure out them in which amount and what degree you should do each of them.

And you repeat the cycle. So Monday you do stretching, then Tuesday you do cardiovascular. Then Wednesday you do strength exercises, or you break it, right, based on whatever is your health plan. So on those lines, what you need to do is you need to break it down. So you have to think of it like a tree where you are at the root. The root is the problem, and then the top reaching the top of the tree is your solution. So basically, you take your first goal, whatever you want to achieve, and then put sub goals under it and to achieve, you decompose it further, you write down your first main goal. Then you write maybe three or four sub goals to achieve the main goal. And then each of the sub goals you write steps to take or tasks to do so that each of the sub goals can be achieved and you can further break it down, but I suggest you break it down at three levels and then it'll be more than enough for you.

So in management terms, it is called as a work breakdown structure. Basically, you break down your work into a tree view and each of your work, each of your node or each of your end leaf becomes the task that you need to complete, and then you can track it in that way. I will tell you an example or one story where I managed one of my works, one of my personal works, using this approach. So, what had happened at that time is my son, he was very much impressed on how golf is played. So he was interested in golf and it was just a initial ignition, basically a small spark where he saw someone playing golf on a golf club. And he said that, what is this golf all about and how I can play it? And he was basically interested in it. So we were just driving somewhere and we had that five minutes conversation where he was asking me about golf and how to play and how to learn more about it.

Speaker 1 (04:29):

So what I did was I told him that that's a very good thing. So give me one day's time and I will explain it to you tomorrow. So on Saturday, what I did was I did some research on golf because I have played golf, but I had not played it from a small passion to a profession perspective right Now. I knew that my son had this ability to take it to a next level, but then I thought that, let me see how I can take a spark and make a fire out of it. So what I did was I started exploring what all things are available on golf. The first thing was there was a golf club nearby my house. The second thing I looked for was there was an application where you can play golf on your mobile phone. And the third thing was of course, a golf book, and fourth thing was a golf TV channel.

So, these four things I identified. So, I wanted to ignite the fire right in my son. So, the first thing I did was I asked him how much interested he was in knowing more about golf. He said, I'm interested. So, then I first thought that I should give him an overview of golf, but I did not want it to be a boring overview. So, I wanted to make sure that I give him enough material, enough food. So, this is a small sprout which has come out of the seed, so let me give enough food to it so that the sprout can grow a bit more. So I took him to a golf course. We just enjoyed and evening war there where I took him to the golf course and ensured that there was a cafe over there. So, we just took

out a hot chocolate and I took a coffee and I said, let's see
how golf course looks and how people play.

So, we just observed it for one hour or so, and we did
not do anything. We just went over there, had a coffee, he
had a nice chocolate, and we just came back. So I did not
discuss anything about it. I just wanted to show him how a
golf course looks. So that was my first sub goal. Then the
second sub goal I actually was, he is also interested in
playing video games. So I told him, okay, I will download a
golf video game for you on my mobile phone. You can
play it for some time maybe for one or two weeks, and tell
me more about it. So instead of me explaining him what
golf means, I gave him a game, but then I monitored it
because children trained, they tend to play more on these
mobile devices and then forget the actual playing, right?
You can actually go and play a thing; they forget about
it. I used to monitor it. I used to give it to him for around
30 minutes or so, maybe by an hour over the weekend. So
that much time only we were allowed to play that
particular game. And after two weeks, again, I did not ask
him about it. I was just giving him, and I did not ask him
even a single question about it. After two weeks, I asked
him, now you tell me what you know about golf. And I
was really amazed that he was knowing everything about it,
what is needed at a starter level. So, he was knowing all the
golf clubs, he was knowing how it is scored. He was
knowing all the terminologies they use in golf. He was also
knowing about what is a birdie, and also knowing about
what is an eagle and what is a condor and how many
people have hit a condor.

So, he was knowing all about it. He had done, his
interest had grown into a bit of big fire, not a very big fire,
but at least a big fire. Then the third step, which I took was
I took him to one of the many golf play area. So you have
these play mini golf adventure golfs in malls or in play

areas or in entertainment centers. So, you can go over
there and buy some golf balls over there or session also.
And then they mostly have 17- or 18-hole course, which is
kind of a fun thing. So, I did that with him, and of course I
tried to ensure that he's guiding me

Stuff. I being a teacher, I asked him to teach me how to
play it, and because he was playing with the app, he knew
about it. So, he was trying his best, and I was a student for
him, and I was again amazed that he was having much
more knowledge about it. Then me, of course, I was not
reading about it, but because his awareness had increased
in those three or four weeks. So then after that we decided
how to score. So, he even took a pencil and a scorecard
and he even marked my scores, and then he showed me
how you play 18-hole golf course and then how it is
scored. And also, he showed me all those things and we
came home and next weekend I took him to a golf driving
range and I told him that let's try it over here.

So, you can hire clubs from there at the golf clubs, and
then you can play over there at the around 70 or 150 balls
to play for 30 minutes or one hour, and you can drive in
that range. So, I did that. So, he said that was a fun activity
for him, and then we did it for around three or four weeks.
So now the fire had grown, right? So now the fire had
grown. So, I was achieving my sub goals. My first sub goal
was to create awareness. I did that by visiting with my son
to a golf course and just had a coffee and chocolate over
there. The second step was to create increase more
awareness. So, I gave him the mobile app. The third thing
was to make the fire more intense. So, I took him to
adventure golf in a mall.

The fourth thing was to see how it actually looks, right?
So, we tried it in a arriving range, and then he came and
asked me one week that, can I have a coach who can teach

me more about it? That was the time when the fire had grown. So, then I had checked around my place and I found a good coach, and that is how the goal journey started. So you have to take it one step at a time. Basically, once you identify a goal, you have to create sub goals and then sub task for all the sub goals, and then you have to achieve it, right? So it's a journey, and journey has to be taken one step at a time. So, as I said earlier, you can either use a sequential model or a model or an agile model.

Key Takeaways:

- When trying to achieve a goal, it is important to break it down into smaller, manageable steps.
- This can be done by creating sub-goals and tasks for each sub-goal.
- The process can be sequential, where each step is completed in order, or agile, where tasks are completed in cycles.
- Breaking down the work into a tree-like structure, known as a work breakdown structure, can help track progress.
- An example of using this approach is given, where a parent helps their child develop an interest in golf by gradually exposing them to different aspects of the sport

Actions You can Implement

1. **Create awareness:** Visit places or engage in activities related to the goal to gain knowledge and understanding.
2. **Provide resources:** Give access to relevant tools, such as mobile apps or books, to further explore and learn about the goal.
3. **Foster interest:** Encourage and support the individual's passion by exposing them to experiences that ignite their

enthusiasm.

4. Set sub-goals: Break down the main goal into smaller, achievable objectives to make progress in a step-by-step manner.

5. Identify tasks: Determine specific actions or tasks that need to be completed to accomplish each sub-goal.

6. Seek guidance: Find a coach, mentor, or expert who can provide guidance and teach necessary skills.

7. Practice and experience: Engage in activities or exercises related to the goal to gain practical experience and improve skills.

8. Monitor progress: Regularly assess and track progress towards the goal to stay motivated and make necessary adjustments.

9. **Use a structured approach:** Consider using a sequential or agile model to plan and execute tasks effectively.

10. Break it down: Use a work breakdown structure to break the overall goal into manageable tasks and track progress.

Activities that can help you

1. **Create awareness:** Visit places or engage in activities related to the goal to gain knowledge and understanding.

2. **Use mobile apps or technology:** Utilize relevant apps or technology to learn and explore more about the goal.

3. **Take practical steps:** Engage in hands-on experiences or activities related to the goal, such as visiting a golf driving range.

4. **Seek guidance or coaching:** Find a coach or mentor who can provide guidance and teach you more about the goal.

5. **Break down the goal:** Create sub-goals and tasks to achieve the main goal, and break them down further into manageable steps.

6. **Track progress:** Keep track of your progress by marking scores or tracking achievements.

7. **Use a sequential or agile approach:** Choose a method that works best for you, whether it's following a step-by-step sequence or using a sprint approach with defined timeframes.

Example Case Study to summit a mountain

1. **Research and gather information about the mountain:** Learn about the mountain's location, elevation, weather conditions, and any specific requirements or permits needed for climbing.

2. **Physical training and preparation:** Engage in regular physical exercise and training to build strength, endurance, and cardiovascular fitness. This may include activities such as hiking, running, weightlifting, and cardio exercises.

3. **Acquire necessary gear and equipment:** Research and obtain the appropriate gear and equipment needed for mountain climbing, such as hiking boots, backpack, climbing ropes, harness, helmet, and appropriate clothing for different weather conditions.

4. **Develop climbing skills and techniques:** Enroll in mountaineering courses or seek guidance from experienced climbers to learn essential climbing skills, techniques, and safety protocols.

5. **Plan and prepare a climbing itinerary: Create** a detailed plan for the climb, including the route, campsites, estimated timeframes, and contingency plans for emergencies or unexpected situations.

6. **Acclimate to high altitudes:** If the mountain has high elevations, it is crucial to acclimate to the altitude gradually to minimize the risk of altitude sickness. This may involve spending time at higher elevations before attempting the summit.

7. **Practice on smaller mountains or hills:** Gain experience and confidence by climbing smaller mountains or hills before attempting a more challenging summit. This allows for skill development and familiarization with the demands of mountain climbing.

8. **Join a guided expedition or climb with experienced climbers**: Consider joining a guided expedition or climbing with experienced climbers who can provide guidance, support, and safety during the climb.

9. **Monitor weather conditions:** Stay updated on weather forecasts and be prepared to adjust plans or postpone the climb if weather conditions are unfavorable or unsafe.

10. **Maintain a positive mindset and perseverance:** Climbing a mountain can be physically and mentally challenging. It is essential to stay motivated, maintain a positive mindset, and persevere through difficulties and setbacks.

6 SIXTH STEP: COMBINE IT ALL TOGETHER

So, this is the story about combine it all together. So, I'm going to tell you about my first visit to Edinburgh. This was back in 2001, somewhere in May or June month. I don't remember exactly, but I was planning to go to Edinburgh and I asked my couple of friends that, are you planning to join me? It was a long weekend, and that is why I planned to go to Edinburgh and visit places around Edinburgh. So, Scotland, Scotland is one of my favorite places to be in. I like to go and spend my time in Scotland because of the very natural, very beautiful nature over there and the nice locks and beautiful mountains over there. So, I like to spend time in Scotland. I wanted to visit Scotland. I had always heard about it. So, this was my first visit to Edinburgh, and what happened is when I asked my couple of friends, are you willing to join me, they said that they were not available because they were already having some plans.

So, what I did is it was about two weeks before I went to Edinburgh, I thought about all the three things, where I'm currently, where I want to go, and how I'm going to travel over there, including the complete itinerary planning. It was a long four days weekend, so I wanted to spend nice time for all the four dates. So what I did was basically I pulled out a sheet of paper and I decided to write it down because if you write it down, it gives you more clarity. So I thought that instead of just keeping it in my mind, let me write it down. So I started writing it down that my end goal is to visit Edinburgh, and then I was living in London, so I had to travel from London to Edinburgh, and on the fourth day, I needed to travel back from Edinburgh to London because I had to work of course, the next day. So then I started thinking on this, and the first problem was to solve how I go from London to Edinburgh and come back from Edinburgh to London, maybe traveling at night so that I will be spending more time over there. So, more time during the day, plus I would be also saving on a hotel. Instead of staying in a hotel, I would be traveling so that two nights I would be saving on the hotel as well. So that was the plan. So, what I did was I traveled to Edinburgh at night.

I was looking for options. The train was quite costly. Of course, the flight was very costly at that time, and I was looking for good deals. And then there was a bus, which was taking a, it was a night bus, I believe, 10 30 or so from the Coast station in London to Edinburgh bus station and back, and it was all under 25 pounds, I believe. So, I said that that was a good deal. I took that deal and the travel time was around seven or eight hours. I don't remember exactly, but the best part of it was I was sitting late evening on Thursday or Friday night, and then I was coming back on Sunday night. So, Monday morning I was back in London, so six o'clock I was back in London and my office started around eight o'clock. So, I was having good two hours to get ready and go to the office.

So that was a very nice itinerary because it was helping me achieve my goal or spending more time in Edinburgh, plus coming back to London on time, and this was all in the night journey. So, six o'clock, I completed my work on the Thursday, and then Friday, Saturday, Sunday, Monday was a holiday. So, I started late in the night. I went to

Victoria and then traveled from there to Edinburgh, and then I had full four days to plan. So, once I did this first level of planning, I decided what I'm going to do on day one. So day one, I decided that I should first go around Edinburgh. So I was traveling in morning to Edinburgh, saw the Royal Mile, then visited one of the gardens, and I also had a look at Edinburg Castle. That was my morning part. And then in the afternoon, I was going to go and spend some time in the tour bus, the open bus where you can take a tour and they'll tell you what all things happened in Edinburgh and they'll tell you about all the important facts and all the important places in the tour.

That was my afternoon plan. And in the evening, I had nice dinner in a hotel, which is offering a deal. So that was again my night plan. So that was my day one. Then for day two, I was planning to go into the Highlands, of course, see the beautiful Highlands. So, I took a guided tour. I forgot the tour name, but it was somewhere based in Edinburgh, and they again had a good deal. So, they had one day tour and two days tour. So, I booked one day tour because I did not know how two days tour would be. So I took one day tour with them. So, they made me visit all the important places. So, there was a Loch Lomond, and then there was some important castles they covered. So that was my second day. On the third day, I explored more and I thought that Inwardness was a good place to go because there was the messy monster and Loch Ness.

I wanted to see Loch Ness also. That was very beautiful lock. So that was on my third day, and on fourth day, I visited again using one day tour. I visited the highest mountain in Britain. That was Ben Navis. And there was also Commando Memorial, which I wanted to visit because it was again, a very beautiful memorial and there was a history behind it. I always like to go to historic places, so I was decided to go over there. So that was my

four days of planning. And now for stay, I was looking at
bed and breakfast at that time. So, I was looking for deals,
and I got two deals. One was in Edinburgh, and second
was again in Edinburgh, but a bit out of Edinburgh, out of
the Edinburgh town city center. So, it was a bit of way. So,
I went over there.

So, when I planned all of this together, I first planned
the start and end how I'm going to do it. Then I planned
each and every day what I'm going to do for each and
every day. And lastly, I planned where I'm going to stay.
And then with this level of planning, when I visited, that
was one of my most memorable trips. It lasted in my
memory forever. I still remember most of the things that I
had done on that trip. I still remember the places I visited
over there. And after that, I have visited Edinburgh three
or four times. I first took my wife when I was married, and
then of course I took my kid again over there to go and
visit at Edinburgh. And both of them loved it. Now
because I had put it all together during my first trip, I really
enjoyed that trip. And because I was aware of what is how
it was there; I was also able to give the same experience to
my family. And they also loved the experience. The
purpose of telling you this story is if you have all the three
things figured, where I am, where I want to go, and
how I'm going to go from where I am to where I am, to

Where want to go, basically from point A to point B,
how I'm going to do it. If you have this all figured
together, if you combine all these three things, believe me,
you'll have a memorable trip. It'll be a memorable time; it'll
be a memorable journey. Whatever dream you have, if you
plan these three things and put them all together, you
cannot think in isolation. You have to think about these
three things together, and you take each and every step
that is needed to go from point A to point B in your life,
then you'll have a wonderful chance of achieving your

goal. The probability of success will be very high. So if you have the end goal in mind, if you know where you are, the current blockers that are there, and then if you plan it properly till the end and follow all the steps, align your plan to the changing situation, then chances are bright that you will achieve your goals.

So that is all what I wanted to tell you through this video, that to achieve things in your life, you need to know where you are, where you want to go, or where you want to be, and how you will be going over there, what changes you'll do to achieve the goal. And you have to combine these all three things together, because if you don't combine all of these three things together, then you won't have a plan, and you would not have the motivation to take the steps that are needed to go from point A to point B, whatever your dream. You have to have these three simple steps that will help you. You have to identify the daily, weekly, monthly actions that you have to take, and then you have to take those actions, and that is how you achieve the goal that you want to achieve.

Key Takeaways:
- The speaker shares their experience of planning a trip to Edinburgh and emphasizes the importance of combining three key elements: knowing where you are, where you want to go, and how you will get there.
- By planning and considering these three factors together, the speaker was able to have a memorable trip and achieve their goal of spending more time in Edinburgh.
- The speaker encourages applying this approach to other areas of life, stating that by having a clear end goal, understanding the current obstacles, and planning the

necessary steps, one can increase their chances of success
in achieving their goals.

Actions You can Implement

1. **Setting specific and measurable targets**:
Clearly define what you want to achieve and
set specific, measurable goals that will help
you track your progress.

2. **Creating a detailed action plan:** Break down
your goals into smaller, manageable tasks and
create a step-by-step plan to accomplish them.

3. **Taking consistent and focused action:**
Commit to taking consistent action towards your
goals, even if it means stepping out of your
comfort zone or facing challenges along the way.

4. **Seeking knowledge and learning:**
Continuously educate yourself and acquire the
necessary skills and knowledge to support your
goals. This may involve reading books, attending
seminars, or taking courses.

5. **Building a strong support system:** Surround
yourself with like-minded individuals who can
provide support, guidance, and accountability as
you work towards your goals.

6. **Embracing failure and learning from it:**
Understand that setbacks and failures are a natural

part of the journey. Learn from them, adapt your approach, and keep moving forward.

7. **Prioritizing and managing your time effectively:** Identify your most important tasks and allocate your time and energy accordingly. Eliminate distractions and focus on high-impact activities.

8. **Taking calculated risks:** Be willing to step outside of your comfort zone and take calculated risks that have the potential to propel you closer to your goals.

9. **Staying motivated and resilient:** Maintain a positive mindset, stay motivated, and develop resilience to overcome obstacles and setbacks.

10. **Celebrating milestones and progress:** Acknowledge and celebrate your achievements along the way to stay motivated and reinforce your commitment to your goals.

Activities that can help you for planning a trip of life

1. Researching and comparing transportation options (train, flight, bus) to find the best deal
2. Planning and booking accommodations (such as bed and breakfast) in advance
3. Creating a detailed itinerary for each day of the trip, including specific attractions and landmarks to visit

4. Booking guided tours or excursions to explore specific areas or attractions (e.g., Highlands, Loch Ness, Ben Nevis)
5. Researching and identifying restaurants or dining options for meals
6. Allowing for flexibility in the plan to adapt to changing situations or unexpected events
7. Taking necessary actions to align the plan with the changing situation
8. **Ensuring** that daily, weekly, and monthly actions are identified and taken to progress towards the goal.

How can above example help me make a million dollars?

Following these actions and activities can help you achieve a million dollars by providing a structured approach to reaching your financial goal. Just like planning a trip, you need to know where you currently stand financially (point A), where you want to be (point B), and how you will get there.

First, assess your current financial situation, including your income, expenses, assets, and liabilities. This will give you a clear understanding of where you are starting from.

Next, set a specific and measurable goal of reaching a million dollars. This will serve as your destination or point B.

Then, create a detailed plan outlining the steps
you will take to achieve your goal. Break it
down into daily, weekly, and monthly actions
that you need to take. This could include
increasing your income, reducing expenses,
investing wisely, and saving consistently.

Consistently follow your plan and make
adjustments as needed to align with changing
circumstances. Stay motivated and committed
to taking the necessary steps to move from
point A to point B.

By combining these three elements - knowing
your current financial situation, setting a
specific goal, and creating a detailed plan - you
increase your chances of achieving your
financial goal of a million dollars. However, it's
important to note that individual results may
vary, and achieving a million dollars requires
discipline, hard work, and smart financial
decisions.

7 SEVENTH STEP: LIST ACTIONS AND TAKE ACTIONS

Okay, so this is story about how to list actions and take the actions on daily basis. So I remember this was in 2009 when I had joined a new company in a new role, and first one week or so I was going under the trainings that are needed for the organization, the mandatory trainings. After the trainings, they put me on a live project and I went and met my manager, my boss. I asked him, it was the first icebreaker meeting. So I asked him what things are there and how the job is and what all things I need to do. It was quite a informal conversation I had with him. And again, I met my team, I met my other colleagues, and basically there was also client introduction. Client was of course not back at my home place. So this was in India. So, client was somewhere in UK.

And at that time, I was working for one of the banks, so they were my client. So, after the first day's icebreakers, the second day, I went to my manager and I'm sitting in front of him and thinking what to talk about. So, he was telling me, okay, welcome Sachin to this project. And he was giving me where things are right currently. And of course,

they had hired me because there was a problem. So
whenever there is a new hiring, there is always a fire that
you have to put down, right? That's why they had hired,
they hired you. So, I was asking him, can you please tell me
what all problems you have or why you have hired me?
What problems should I be solving? And he was really
impressed because no one had asked him this direct
question. He was working with so many colleagues the
first day, no one had asked them this basic question that
why you hired me and what is the fire that I need to put
off?

He said that you're right. I have hired you because there is
a fire, there is a fire, there is a problem, and I need your
experience, your help to solve the problem. So, then he
explained me the situation. I took all the notes. I was not
interrupting him. I did not ask any questions because I like
people to talk. And when they talk, they give you more
pointers to what things are. So, I just spent two hours with
him understanding what was his perspective of things and
where the problem were according to him. And then I
wrote it all down. And what I did was I had another
meeting with him after two days and I told him that this is
what I understand because I did not give him any
questions. I mean not ask him any questions on the first
day. So, I told him that this is what I understand and if you
think I'm wrong in any of my understandings, please
correct me.

And then I presented him around 30 minutes or so, what
all problems I thought were there, what all fires were there,
and what all fires he had hired me to put what all fires
were there. So basically, whatever he had told me based on
that information, I had put a summary of it around 20 or
points I had put. And I asked him whether these are valid.
So he said that, yes, these are valid ones, but out of that,
around six or seven were incorrectly understood. So he
explained me those again and then he said, what are you

going to do about it? So I said, give me one day's time. I
will think about something. And in terms of fixing this
problem, before coming to solutions, what I did was I
listed those 15 one-liners. I went to the team members and
I asked them that these are the 15 things which I'm being
told are problems.

So, what is you are understanding on this? I asked this
question to my team members and some of them agreed to
it. Some of them did not agree to it. So, whatever was the
agreement, whatever was their understanding. Based on
that, I again revised the 15 one-liners and expanded them a
bit because I had now more information about it. And
then I went to client, there was a client meeting, so we had
the initial introduction and all. So, they were asking me
about my experience and all, and then they said that, do
you have any questions? So, I told them that yes, I have a
lot of questions and these are my 15 points, which I have
put expanded into three or four lines. And what is your
thought on it or what do you think, whether I'm correct,
whether I'm wrong, can you please validate these?

So, client also gave me their inputs. And based on those
inputs, I prepared a brief summary for each. So now that
three or four liners had become one page summary. So I
had around 15 odd pages, a bit of summary written on all
the problems that are there, which I was hired to be
solving or to be at least give it a try. And after that, what
happened was all these problems were documented. So, all
these 15 one pager summaries were documented, and then
I again validated it with all the three important
stakeholders, my manager, my team, and my client. And
once I validated them all, I knew that this is the problem.
So, I took around two or three weeks to do this exercise. I
spent more time on the diagnosis, right? If you have more
correct understanding of the problem, and then you can
propose solutions.

And then second activity, which I did was I again, connected with all these three people. I gave them my perspective that how I would solve those problems. And I also took their perspective, what are their inputs to solve the problems? And again, based on that, I prepared a small report out of it for each of the 15 problems. And then we knew the problem, we knew the solution, it might not be the best solution, but at least we knew where to start. And then what I did after that was I again took the solution and put it into a task, a task list. Basically, you have to implement the solution with one step at a time. So, I list down all the actions, the owners of the actions and a tentative date by which that action should be taken. So, I put them in sequence and I identified another thing was which of those were recurring actions on what was the recurring frequency, whether they were recurring daily, monthly, weekly.

So based on that, I put the complete task list. And then I said, I educated my manager and my team about the task list. Also took their inputs. I corrected some of the tasks, the owners, and then the timeline as well, because some of the tasks, my understanding might have been wrong. So whatever time it took to complete that task, I revise that as well. And then we all together, my client, my team, my manager and me, we all together went to client and gave them the proposal that these are the 15 problems. These are the solutions that we are thinking based on current situation or current understanding. And these are the tasks that we are going to do to take the action and implement the solutions. And once I had done that, what happened was clients' confidence in our work increased. They gave us, of course, their inputs that some of the tasks needs to be changed or some of the timelines have to be moved, whatever inputs they had. So accordingly, with made regions to it. And we came up with a live plan. And after that, my daily job was very simple, open a group chat every day, put all the tasks that are there for that particular day, for that particular week, and check the status where it is and wherever there were delays. So, each task was marked in red, amber,

Or green. So whichever task were red or amber, where there are dealers or problems, I used to jump in and try to help people with the problem. So, I was becoming more of a problem solver. And then at the end of the day, I used to just take the report and send it out to my manager, my client, that this is the current progress. And after three or four months out of those 15 problems, I believe 13, they're gone. Two of them, we had implemented the wrong solution. So, we corrected that and those were again gone in next two, three months. So, the whole thing, what we did was we had a plan in place where there were tasks broken down into owners and deadlines and the tracking of the tasks. And then what I realized was if I apply the same principle for any goal, if I list down actions that are needed to achieve a goal, to go from point A to point B, whatever steps I need to take, if I put them as task with a deadline, with a timeline, and track it to closure. Now when I said to closure means the activity has to be completed. If there are delays, then you have to understand where the delays are and resolve those delays. So try to solve them, take an alternate path, do whatever is needed to take care of the task.

So once I did that, I was able to completely deliver the goals or achieve the goals that we had initially planned. And some of the goals I was not able to achieve. So I had done a correction out to it. The planning was changed to replanning. We had a replanning exercise, and after re-planning, after adjusting, we were able to achieve the goals. So the same thing applies to all the goals in life. Whatever goals are there, you have to think of the goals, where you want to go, you have to think where you are, you have to know how to achieve all the things. So basically, how you're going to do go from point A to point B, you have to put it all together. All the three things have to be combined. Break them down into task, have each task owner a deadline, a timeline by which it needs to be completed, and a status in terms of red, amber, or green.

So, if it is green, means it's on track. If it's amber, it might slip. And if it's red, it means it has already slipped. So for amber and red, you take the corrective actions, the correct actions that will bring the plan back on track. And that is how you can achieve the goal. That is how you can list all the actions, all tasks, complete the task, and then track them to closure. That is what I mean by closure. So basically, completing the task from start to finish with whatever is needed to finish the task is closure of it. And you have to do this tracking on daily basis because if you do it on daily basis only then whether you are on the target or you are moving off the target. So, this will help you to achieve whatever goal you have. And then consistency and regular checks will help you to achieve the goal within the timeframe that you have in your mind. So that is all about this story, listing actions and taking the massive actions that will really help.

Key Takeaways:
- When starting a new project or job, it is important to understand the problems or challenges that need to be addressed.
- Asking direct questions about the problems and goals can impress managers and provide valuable insights.
- Taking the time to thoroughly understand the problems and gather input from team members and clients is crucial for effective problem-solving.
- Breaking down the problems into actionable tasks with

owners, deadlines, and timelines helps create a clear plan of action.

- Regular tracking and monitoring of tasks, along with addressing any delays or issues, is essential for achieving goals.

- Adjustments and replanning may be necessary along the way, but consistent effort and regular checks can lead to successful goal achievement.

Actions to be taken on new job/assignment

1. The speaker joined a new company and asked their manager about the problems they were hired to solve.

2. The speaker spent time understanding the problems and validating their understanding with stakeholders.

3. They then developed solutions and created a task list with actions, owners, and deadlines.

4. The speaker regularly tracked the progress of tasks and made adjustments as needed.

5. By consistently taking action and tracking progress, the speaker was able to solve most of the problems and achieve their goals.

6. The key takeaway is to list actions, assign owners and deadlines, and track progress to achieve goals effectively.

Case Study of Meeting Health Goal

Yes, this approach to problem-solving and goal achievement can definitely help someone in their personal growth. Let's take an example:

Imagine a person named Sarah who wants to improve her physical fitness and overall health. She applies the same principle mentioned in the context to achieve her goal.

First, Sarah lists down her actions that are needed to achieve her goal, such as going to the gym, eating a balanced diet, and getting enough sleep. She breaks down these actions into smaller tasks with deadlines and timelines. For example, she sets a goal to go to the gym three times a week, cook healthy meals at home, and get at least 7 hours of sleep every night.

Sarah tracks her progress on a daily basis, marking each task as red, amber, or green. If she is on track with her actions, she marks them as green. If she is slightly off track, she marks them as amber and takes corrective actions to get back on track. And if she completely misses a task, she marks it as red and finds alternative solutions to complete it.

By consistently following this approach and regularly checking her progress, Sarah is able to achieve her fitness and health goals within the timeframe she has set for herself. She stays motivated and accountable by tracking her actions and making necessary adjustments along the way.

This approach not only helps Sarah in achieving her physical fitness goals but also promotes personal growth by instilling discipline, time management skills, and problem-solving abilities. It allows her to break down her goals into manageable tasks, stay focused, and take consistent action towards her desired outcome.

How can above story help me grow my business?

This approach to problem-solving and goal achievement can help you grow your business by providing a structured and organized way to tackle challenges and achieve your objectives. Here's how it can be applied:

1. **Identify and prioritize problems:** Just like in the story, start by identifying the problems or challenges your business is facing. Prioritize them based on their impact on your business.

2. **Break down goals into actionable tasks:** Once you have identified the problems, break down your goals into specific, actionable tasks. Assign owners and deadlines to each task to ensure accountability.

3. **Track progress and take corrective actions**: Regularly track the progress of each task and identify any delays or issues. Take corrective actions to bring the plan back on track. This will help you stay focused and ensure that you are making progress towards your goals.

4. **Replan and adjust as needed**: If you encounter obstacles or realize that your initial plan needs adjustment, be open to replanning and making necessary changes. This flexibility will allow you to adapt to new circumstances and find alternative solutions.

5. **Involve stakeholders and seek feedback:** Engage your team, clients, and other stakeholders in the problem-solving and goal achievement process. Seek their input and feedback to gain different perspectives and improve the quality of your solutions.

6. **Consistency and regular checks**: Maintain consistency in tracking progress and checking the status of

tasks. Regularly review and evaluate your progress to ensure that you are on track and making the necessary adjustments.

By following this approach, you can effectively address challenges, achieve your goals, and ultimately grow your business.

8 EIGHTH STEP: REVIEW EVERY WEEK

So, this is a story about review your work every week. So why it is important to review your work every week. I remember this time when I was in college in my last year of the graduation, and one of my teachers tells me that the most successful person in this world is not the one who is more creative, is not the one who is richer, is not the one who has knowledge or some special skills, is not the person who is most disciplined, but is the person who is more regular. No, I was amazed to hear that why a regular person can always be successful. Then my professor told me the story, right? So I asked him, can you please explain me this more why a regular person is more successful? So he tells me, listen, my friend, the regular person is the one who takes action on regular basis.

So, there is a story about Bruce Lee and what Bruce Lee says is, I'm not afraid about a person who knows kung fu, where he can kick in 20 different ways, or he practices 20 different types of kicks every day. But I'm afraid of a person who practices the same kick 20 times every day. So, it took me a bit time to understand this, right? I'm not afraid of a person who knows 20 different kicks, but I'm afraid of a person who knows one kick and practices it 20 times a day. So, I believe that is the definition of a regular. If you repeatedly do a task on a regular basis, on a frequent basis, then you'll eventually get it. That's why reviewing your work on every week is very important. So how do you review your work? Basically, review your work. Should I only have three questions and three answers? What were my planned activities for last week? What is the current status of each of these activities and what are my planned activities for next week? If you answer these three questions every week, say about one or two hours, then it'll help you to monitor your progress.

So, I'll tell you another story where I was working as a project leader at that time for one of the organizations, and that is the first time when I started conducting a status meeting with my team and with my client and with my manager. So, they told me, the management told me that we need a regular status report from you on a weekly basis on where the project is and what is happening with it, and what are the areas where you need help from management or which all things you need to get escalated. Basically, what tasks are in red, what task are in amber and what task in green and what are the corrective and preventive actions? Now, when I say corrective and preventive actions, let me add to that, corrective action is the one where you have done a mistake and whatever harm or whatever damage that mistake has caused, you need to correct it.

So that action is called as corrective action. While a preventive action is one which stops you from making the same mistake again. So, you go and fix the root cause and you prevent that mistake from happening again. So that is the definition of corrective and preventive actions. So, I was told about preparing a status report every week, and it was, I believe a PowerPoint slide, and it only had three sections in it. First was highlights and lowlights for the

week. Second was task and status for last week, and third
was plan, task for next week. So, what I did was basically
you saw the template and then I went to my manager and
asked him, can you please explain me what is this
highlights and lowlights and what is this plan activities for
next week and what is the status for this week? How do I
fill it because there are so many activities over here and
you are asking me to give me it in one slide, right?
(04:59):
Like a snapshot. So, he told me very important thing, he
said, you have to list down five or maybe eight, five to
eight key activities for the week, and then take the status of
which and the owner and the date. So basically, if you can
see it as a table, it is a very simple table. It has a column
called as the task name. Then second is the status. So red,
amber, green. Then it has a end date or a deadline and
owner. So those are only four columns in the task list.
Then highlights and lowlights for current week. So,
highlights mean whatever positive things or what are good
things that you have achieved for the current week. So,
what all things

You have achieved towards your goal. That will be your
highlights, maybe around three highlights, and then low
lights, if any. So, when I say if any, there may not be any
low lights. Typically, there are low lights. So low lights are
basically what all things there you have failed in this week.
So, it is okay to fail, but you need to list down your
failures. And as I repeated earlier, as I said earlier, you have
to take the corrective and prevent your actions on the
failure. So that's why the low lights and then for next week,
what all activities are planned. So, everyone knows what all
activities are planned. So, I thought that, okay, this is a
very nice status report and if I can use it in my personal
goals, let me see if it helps me. And I started preparing that
for my personal goals as well.

And my personal goals were divided into three categories. What are my health goals? What are my relationship goals, and what are my career or financial goals? So top two goals for each. So around six to seven tasks and the status of each. So red, amber, green, whether it's on track, the deadline, and the owner. Now owner in this case was mostly me, but sometimes I used to put joint ownership, like if I was joining a gym or if I was inviting a friend for a mountain walk over that week, maybe for my health goal. So, I used to put that person's name over there along with me so that if you have another person, it creates accountability and then highlights. I was putting at highlight kind of 10,000 steps, walked every day for four or five days a week. Then in terms of my career goals, it was learned a new module or read a new book related to my project work or related to my career. And in terms of relationships, it was of course taking out a loved one to a party or appreciated someone or written an appreciation note later apologized to someone. Those were kind of things which I was doing in relationships, small things, but they do big wins.

So those things I was preparing on weekly basis and then for next week, whatever was planned health goal, relationship goal, and the financial or the career goal. So I used to list this and when I started preparing simple one slider or one pager, and it got collected over a couple of weeks, so I had around eight or 10 weeks of data, and then I was able to plot it, right? If you have eight or 10 data points and you just put it in Excel sheet, then you can create a graph out of it. So it was telling me how I am trending in terms of my health goals, how I was trending in terms of my relationship goals, and how I was trending in terms of my financial or my career goals. So once a trend line is there, then it gives you a visual picture of your life.

So that is how it helped me and that is how I prepared this weekly status of me. And on regular basis, I used to review what all things I'm doing in all my goals and where I am lacking and where I'm improving. And accordingly, I used to take the corrective and preventive actions. So saying that other thing which I regularly do is I keep this activity towards the end of the week because towards the end of the week, like Friday or Saturday or Max, you can delayed by Sunday. And I used to do this early in the morning, Friday morning or Saturday morning or Sunday morning because then I knew where I need to spend more efforts. And if you do it early in the morning, it is a better thing for two things. First is early in the morning you have got good mood and you are fresh, right?

And second is you don't forget it. If you do it early in the morning, the task is completed. So the status weekly self status is completed. Now I look at this self status or self review or weekly review, whatever you want to call it as a reflection in the mirror. Now, when you have a reflection in the mirror, you don't blame the reflection, right? But you take care of your image. So if you are having shabby hair, then you don't go and comb the image, but you comb your hair and then the image automatically corrects itself. So basically if you know what the current weak picture about yourself is in terms of your goals, then you can take the needed action to improve. But unless and until you know how your reflection looks, you cannot improve because you don't know where to improve. That is why this weekly review weekly status, whatever you want to call it, as I said, is very important action that you need to take because it'll tell you how much more energy you need to put to align yourself towards your goals.

And again, as I said, if you are flying a very big plane, you cannot simply turn 180 degrees. You need to turn maybe five degrees or 10 degrees at a time, and you'll have to do it enough number of times so that you take the complete 180 degree turn. So you have to change your life, but you can do that in increments. But at the same time, if you don't do the increments for long time enough, there is no improvement in your life. So you don't stop after three or four increments. You do it on weekly basis for a very long time, at least three

Months, six months, one year, and then you can see the results. Then you can see that how many goals you have achieved and how much you have improved. So that is all about weekly review every week and the importance of it.

Key Takeaways:
- Regularly reviewing your work is important for success.
- Consistency and taking action on a regular basis is more important than being creative, rich, or disciplined.
- Bruce Lee's philosophy of practicing one kick 20 times a day applies to being regular in your work.
- Reviewing your work can be done by answering three questions: planned activities for last week, current status of each activity, and planned activities for next week.
- Conducting regular status meetings and preparing status reports can help monitor progress and identify areas for improvement.
- The status report should include highlights, lowlights, and planned activities for the week.
- Reviewing personal goals using a similar format can provide insights and help track progress.
- Taking corrective and preventive actions based on the review helps improve performance.
- Reviewing work should be done at the end of the week, preferably in the morning, to have a fresh perspective and ensure completion.
- Weekly reviews serve as a reflection in the mirror,

allowing you to identify areas for improvement and take necessary actions.
- Making incremental changes consistently over time leads to significant improvements in life and goal achievement.

Examples of activities that can be included in the weekly review are:

1. Listing down planned activities for the previous week.

2. Assessing the current status of each activity.

3. Identifying highlights and lowlights of the week.

4. Reflecting on progress towards goals in different areas (health, relationships, career/financial).

5. Taking note of any corrective and preventive actions needed.

6. Setting planned activities for the upcoming week.

7. Reviewing task deadlines and ownership.

8. Evaluating the status of tasks using a red, amber, green (RAG) system.

9. Reflecting on personal achievements and failures.

10. Assessing the overall trend and progress over time.

How you can use Weekly Review in your Life?

Let's say someone has set personal goals in three categories: health, relationships, and career/financial. They decide to review their progress on a weekly basis using a similar format as mentioned in the context.

For the health goals, they list down specific activities such as exercising, eating healthy, and getting enough sleep. They assign a status (red, amber, green) to each activity based on their progress. For example, if they exercised for 4 days out of 7, they might mark it as amber. They also set a deadline for each activity and assign themselves as the owner.

In the highlights section, they note the positive things they achieved towards their health goals. It could be something like consistently hitting their step count target or trying a new healthy recipe. In the lowlights section, they acknowledge any areas where they fell short, such as skipping workouts or indulging in unhealthy snacks.

For the next week, they plan their activities for health goals. It could include specific workouts, meal plans, or health-related appointments. They repeat this process for their relationship and career/financial goals as well.

How can below exercise help you grow?

Consistently reviewing your work and setting goals using this format can help you grow in several ways:

1. **Self-awareness:** By regularly reviewing your work and progress, you gain a deeper understanding of your strengths, weaknesses, and areas for improvement. This self-awareness allows you to make more informed decisions and take targeted actions to enhance your skills and performance.

2. **Goal alignment:** Setting clear goals and regularly reviewing them helps you stay focused and aligned with your long-term objectives. It ensures that your daily actions and tasks are contributing to your overall growth

and success.

3. **Accountability:** The process of reviewing your work and setting goals holds you accountable for your actions. It helps you track your progress, identify any deviations or obstacles, and take corrective measures to stay on track.

4. **Continuous improvement:** By consistently reviewing your work, you can identify patterns, trends, and areas where you can improve. This allows you to make incremental changes and adjustments over time, leading to continuous growth and development.

5. **Motivation and momentum:** Regularly reviewing your work and progress can provide a sense of accomplishment and motivation. It helps you celebrate your achievements, no matter how small, and keeps you motivated to keep pushing forward towards your goals.

Overall, consistently reviewing your work and setting goals using this format provides a structured framework for personal and professional growth. It helps you stay focused, accountable, and continuously improve, leading to long-term success and fulfillment.

Case Study

Let's take an example of someone who consistently reviews their work and sets goals using the format mentioned.

Imagine a person named Sarah who decides to implement this weekly review and goal-setting process in her life. She divides her goals into three categories: health, career, and relationships.

In the health category, Sarah sets a goal to exercise for at least 30 minutes every day. She tracks her progress and updates the status in her weekly review. Initially, she struggles to consistently meet this goal and often marks it as "red" in her status. However, by reviewing her progress every week, she realizes that she needs to make adjustments to her schedule and find ways to stay motivated. She starts waking up earlier and finds a workout buddy to hold her accountable. Over time, her status changes to "amber" and eventually to "green" as she successfully incorporates regular exercise into her routine. This consistent review and goal-setting process helps Sarah improve her health and fitness levels.

In the career category, Sarah sets a goal to learn a new skill relevant to her job every month. She tracks her progress and updates the status in her weekly review. Initially, she finds it challenging to find time for learning amidst her busy schedule. However, by consistently reviewing her progress, she realizes that she needs to prioritize her professional development. She starts dedicating specific time slots each week for learning and seeks out online courses and resources. As she continues to review her progress, she notices that her status changes from "red" to "amber" and eventually to "green" as she acquires new skills and knowledge. This consistent review and goal-setting process helps Sarah enhance her professional growth and opens up new opportunities in her career.

In the relationships category, Sarah sets a goal to spend quality time with her family and friends at least once a week. She tracks her progress and updates the status in her weekly review. Initially, she struggles to balance her personal and professional commitments, often neglecting her relationships. However, through consistent review, she realizes the importance of nurturing her connections. She starts prioritizing family and friend gatherings, scheduling regular outings, and expressing appreciation and gratitude. As she continues to review her progress, she notices that her status changes from "red" to "amber" and eventually to "green" as she strengthens her relationships and creates meaningful connections. This consistent review and goal-setting process helps Sarah foster personal growth and deepen her bonds with loved ones.

By consistently reviewing her work and setting goals using this format, Sarah experiences personal and professional growth in various aspects of her life. She becomes more disciplined, focused, and accountable, leading to positive changes and improvements in her health, career, and relationships.

Planning a Moon Habitat Case Study

The strategies mentioned can help in planning a moon habitat by providing a structured approach to setting goals, tracking progress, and making necessary adjustments. Here's how these strategies can be applied:

1. Identify key activities: List down the key activities required for establishing and maintaining a moon habitat. This could include tasks like constructing the habitat, ensuring life support systems, conducting scientific research, etc.

2. Set goals and deadlines: Assign specific goals and deadlines to each activity. This helps in creating a timeline for the project and ensures that progress is being made

within the desired timeframe.

3. Track status: Use a simple table or spreadsheet to track the status of each activity. This can be done by using a color-coded system like red, amber, and green to indicate whether the activity is behind schedule, on track, or completed.

4. Ownership and accountability: Assign owners to each activity, whether it's individuals or teams responsible for its completion. This helps in creating accountability and ensures that everyone is aware of their responsibilities.

5. Highlight achievements and failures: Record the highlights and lowlights of each week. This allows for celebrating successes and identifying areas where improvements are needed. It's important to learn from failures and take corrective and preventive actions.

6. Plan for the future: Outline the activities planned for the next week or period. This helps in maintaining a forward-looking approach and ensures that the project stays on track.

7. Regular review: Conduct a weekly review of the progress made, areas of improvement, and any necessary adjustments. This review can be done individually or as a team to ensure that everyone is aligned and working towards the common goal.

By following these strategies, the planning and execution of a moon habitat project can be organized, monitored, and adjusted as needed, leading to a higher chance of success.

ABOUT THE AUTHOR

Sachin Medhi is a project manager delivering IT projects and programs for last 17 years. He has worked in organizations like Larsen & Toubro Infotech Limited, Wipro, Cognizant, and Kale Consultants Ltd. He has led multi-million dollar projects from domains as Airlines-Cargo, Banking, Auto and Home Insurance, Re-Insurance, Manufacturing and Logistics. He has worked with clients in countries like UK, USA, Republic of Ireland, South East Asia, and continental Europe. Sachin is a Bachelor in Computer Engineering from prestigious Pune University, Pune, India, certified Project Management Professional (PMP) from PMI, certified Six Sigma Green Belt from American Society for Quality, and a certified Tao Hands Practitioner and Healer from Tao Academy, Toronto. He lives in Belfast, Northern Ireland and spends his leisure time hiking with his son Kaveesh and wife, Amruta. He loves to offer healing to others for their physical, emotional, and financial challenges. His also enjoys connecting with inner-self and universe using spiritual practices for deeper knowledge and wisdom.

Printed in Great Britain
by Amazon

37810084R00050